CLIMATE CHANGE
Simple things you can do
to make a difference

Climate Change

Simple things you can do to make a difference

JON CLIFT & AMANDA CUTHBERT

green books

333/
72

First published in 2008 by
Green Books
Foxhole, Dartington
Totnes, Devon TQ9 6EB
www.greenbooks.co.uk

© Green Books 2008

Printed in the UK by Cambrian Printers, Aberystwyth. The text paper is made from 100% recycled post-consumer waste, and the covers from 75% recycled material.

DISCLAIMER: The advice in this book is believed to be correct at the time of printing, but the authors and publishers accept no liability for actions inspired by this book.

ISBN 978 1 900322 24 9

CONTENTS

Introduction

INTRODUCTION

What is Climate Change?

'Climate Change' is the changing of the world's climate as a result of what we, the humans on this planet, are doing.

It's a massive problem, and in many people's eyes the single biggest problem ever to face humankind; because if we carry on behaving as we're doing now, we face large rises in global temperatures and also in sea levels, which will have disastrous consequences.

There's plenty we can all do to slow it down. Yes, it is a massive challenge, and a topic that's surrounded by loads of gloom and doom, but fortunately we still have time.

This is not one of those scare stories that pop up now and again in the papers – this is real. So much so that ever since 1988 the United Nations has had a team of about 3,000 scientists from all over the world monitoring what is happening, researching what to do about it and advising the world's governments.

'Climate Change' and 'Global Warming' both refer to the same thing, although 'Climate Change' is a better description because the warming up of the earth changes our whole climate, including how much it rains, the strength of the wind, when and how much it snows, and the frequency and strength of storms.

What causes it?

The main cause of climate change is carbon dioxide, a gas that is produced whenever we burn fossil fuels like oil (in the form of petrol or diesel), gas or coal. We use these fuels to give us the energy that we use every day. Power stations burn fuel to make electricity for our homes. We burn fossil fuels to move our cars, buses, trains and planes, to warm our houses, to manufacture our goods – the list is virtually endless.

When fossil fuels are burned, carbon dioxide (CO_2) goes into the atmosphere where, as we burn more and more fossil fuels to feed our ever increasing demand for energy, the amount of CO_2 gas increases. CO_2 has always been in the atmosphere, trapping just enough heat for life on earth. Now this excess of CO_2 has upset this delicate balance, and not enough heat can escape back into space.

Consequently the temperature of our world is slowly but surely rising, and will continue to do so unless we do something about it.

Our homes produce over 1/4 of the UK's CO_2 emissions – even more than our cars.

What proof is there?

We have all been experiencing more extremes of weather recently. Ever since the world's scientists realised that the world was warming, they have been monitoring what has been going on, and the proof is now staring us in the face:

- The average surface temperature of the earth, together with air and sea temperatures, is rising. We can see this because glaciers are retreating, and in some cases disappearing altogether.

- The ice caps at the north and south poles are melting.

- Snow and ice, which for millennia has covered large areas of frozen land, is now rapidly melting.

- Eleven of the last twelve years have been the warmest years ever since records were kept.

- Storms and floods are increasing in intensity and ferocity, with disastrous consequences. Weather patterns are much less predictable than they used to be.

- Flowers are blooming earlier, and some foreign birds are no longer returning home in the winter.

How will climate change affect me?

The world's scientists predict that, unless we dramatically reduce our CO_2 emissions, the temperature of the earth will spiral out of control. This is not going to happen overnight, but things could change far more rapidly than many people expect. The pleasant picture of the UK merely being a little warmer and all of us living a comfortable Mediterranean existence is, unfortunately, not what is on the cards.

Summer temperatures will continue to rise, becoming life-threatening at times. Seriously heavy rainfall and consequently extensive flooding is also expected. Flooding and storm damage will also become more frequent in coastal communities, as sea levels rise and storms increase in ferocity.

In the longer term, as the ice sheets continue to melt, we could face large sea level rises. The ice sheets melting on Greenland alone will probably raise sea levels by six or seven metres, with obvious huge repercussions for many cities and areas which are by or near the coast.

Water supplies will be under duress, with water shortages becoming acute in some parts of the world. This lack of water to both drink and grow crops will, combined with the flooding, create food shortages and force people to move. Large scale migration is expected, placing huge social and political pressure on the host countries.

With the ice melting and the sea warming, sea levels are rising at a rate of about 3mm a year.

What can I do about it?

Now for the good news – there's lots you can do

Most of the world's climate scientists believe we have time to prevent climate change spiralling out of control if we act now. Within the next ten years we all need to dramatically reduce our CO_2 emissions in order to minimise the impact of climate change. It won't be easy – we will need to change our lifestyles – but it is very achievable. Little things that we can do every day can produce large results.

Our electricity consumption has gone up 70% since 1970.

If we all turned off our TVs and other gadgets that are kept on stand-by, for example, we could shut down a couple of power stations in the UK, with huge reductions in CO_2 emissions.

We are all using more and more energy: keeping our rooms so hot that we walk around in short sleeves in the winter, driving the car just around the corner to get the Sunday paper, popping on a plane for a long weekend abroad in the sun, buying French beans in January that have been flown in from Kenya – the list is endless. We need to be more efficient in the way we use energy.

Simple actions can considerably reduce our energy consumption and our energy bills, and help reduce climate change: the less energy we use, the less CO_2 is released, which benefits us all. Once we are aware of what's happening, most of the things we need to do are just common sense.

We don't have to shiver in unheated houses with no modern appliances, or sell our cars and go back to horses and carts; we just have to reduce our carbon footprint.

Climate change terms

Carbon footprint

Your carbon footprint is the measure of the amount of carbon dioxide your activities add to the atmosphere. Surprisingly, many items – from apples to cars – can have a carbon footprint too, especially if they have been flown thousands of miles or if energy has been used in their production. Your purchasing choices can make a big difference to your overall carbon footprint.

Carbon offsetting

Can't I simply pay for somebody to plant a few trees to cancel my CO_2 emissions? Whilst in theory this may seem like a good idea, this process, known as 'carbon offsetting', is unfortunately not the way out of the problem.

The theory of carbon offsetting is based on the concept of allowing CO_2 to be emitted now, and then reducing it at a later date. Carbon offsetting generally involves paying a company either to invest in renewable energy projects which may reduce CO_2 emissions in the future, or to plant trees which will possibly take CO_2 out of the atmosphere at some future date. But the problem of excess CO_2 is here today: we can't afford to wait, and need to work in the present.

The setting up off these 'offsetting' projects creates the perception that we can carry on polluting as we are currently doing, and buy our way out of the problem. It is infinitely preferable to cut emissions in the first place.

Greenhouse gases

These are gases such as carbon dioxide and methane, which accumulate in the atmosphere and prevent heat escaping into space – they act like a greenhouse around the earth. They are being produced in ever-increasing quantities by our activities.

HOME HEATING

What's my heating got to do with climate change?

- When coal, gas or oil are burned to warm your house, carbon dioxide (CO_2) is emitted into the atmosphere; this is the main cause of climate change.

- Coal, gas or oil are burned in power stations to produce the electricity used to warm your home.

Less energy used for heating = less CO_2

What can I do about it?

NOW...

We spend two-thirds of our household energy bills on keeping our homes warm in winter.

- **Take charge of your heating** – how about turning down the thermostat by $1^{\circ}C$ – this can reduce your energy consumption by 10%.

- **Turn radiators off or down** in rooms you only use occasionally.

- **Turn down the thermostat** when you are going away; $5^{\circ}C$ will prevent pipes bursting in cold weather.

- **Set the timer for your heating system** to come on about 30 minutes before you get up or come home in the evening, and to go off about half an hour before you leave in the morning or go to bed.

> **WARNING** – if you are elderly or infirm, try to keep your room temperatures at 18^{0}C at least, and your living room and bathroom at about 21^{0}C.

- **Put on more clothes** rather than turning up the heat.
- **Draw curtains over windows at night**: they provide insulation and help to keep the heat in the room. Avoid covering radiators with curtains – they will funnel the heat out through the glass of the windows.

LATER . . .
- **Buy and fit draught excluders** to your letterboxes, doors and windows. They don't cost much and make a big difference. You may not want to do this in your bathroom or kitchen if you have problems with condensation. Make sure you still have sufficient ventilation.

> **WARNING** – Don't block up air vents or grilles in walls If you have an open gas fire, a boiler with an open flue, or a solid fuel fire or heater. These need sufficient ventilation to burn properly, as otherwise highly poisonous carbon monoxide gas is released.

- **Stop draughts coming under skirting boards or through floorboards** by filling the gaps with strips of wood, cork, or the correct sealant. Make sure you still have sufficient ventilation.

- **Service your boiler regularly** – it will be more efficient and use less energy.

If they're not insulated, almost 40% of all the heat used to warm rooms escapes through the walls and roof space.

- **Insulate your loft**. This is probably one of the simplest and most effective methods of reducing your heat and energy loss. Loft insulation should be a minimum of 270mm thick. You can do it yourself. There are some very user-friendly materials available, but whichever insulation type you choose, protect yourself with appropriate clothing and a face mask. There will probably be a grant available to help you pay for the installation.

- **Insulate your walls**. If you have cavity walls, they are easy and quick to insulate, and in most cases it can be done in a day. Solid walls are insulated by placing cladding either inside or outside; it's more complex, but worthwhile, as solid walls lose more heat than cavity walls. There will probably be a grant available to help you pay for this.

- **Get you electricity from a green supplier** – one that doesn't generate electricity using fossil fuels. See www.greenelectricity.org

If you do just one thing:
TURN DOWN YOUR THERMOSTAT

Water Heating

WATER HEATING

What has my hot water got to do with climate change?

- When you use gas or oil to heat your water, carbon dioxide (CO_2) is produced; this is the main cause of climate change.

- When you use electricity to heat your water, the power station burned coal, gas or oil to produce that electricity – emitting CO_2 in the process.

Less energy used for heating water = less CO_2

What can I do about it?

NOW...

Don't keep your immersion heater on all the time – it's cheaper and consumes less energy if water is heated only when needed.

- **Turn down the temperature of your hot water** at the central heating boiler, at the immersion tank (if your water is heated by electricity), or on your instant water heater.

- **Don't waste energy heating water** only to have to add cold water so that it is not too hot to use! 60°C is ideal.

- **Take a quick shower rather than a bath** – if you use a power shower, remember that in five minutes it can use as much hot water as a bath.

- **Don't leave hot water taps running** – use the plug.

- **Bath with a friend** – you'll use less hot water!

LATER . . .

- **Fix leaking hot water taps** as soon as you can.

- **Buy a timer for your immersion heater**. Set it so that the water is only heated when you need it.

Water heated by an electric immersion heater costs more than 45p an hour. Just turn it on half an hour before you need it – and don't forget to turn it off afterwards!

- **Buy an insulating jacket** if your immersion or hot water tank is not insulated. If you have no jacket, about three-quarters of the energy you are buying to heat your hot water is wasted. Insulating jackets are not expensive – buy one that's at least 75mm thick.

- **Insulate your hot water pipes**. Insulation is cheap and easy to fit: just clip it around your pipes.

If you do just one thing:
KEEP YOUR SHOWERS SHORT

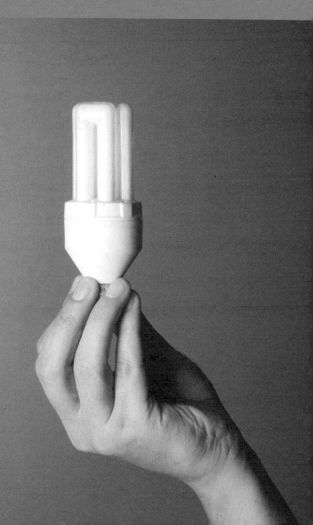

LIGHTING

What has my lighting got to do with climate change?

- When you turn on the light you use electricity from a power station.

- Currently almost three-quarters of all the electricity we generate in the UK is produced in power stations, which burned gas, oil & coal to produce that electricity – emitting CO_2 in the process.

Less lights on = less CO_2

What can I do about it?

NOW...

We spend 10% of our electricity bills on lighting.

- **Get in the habit of turning lights off** when they are not needed.

- **Use natural light** where possible.

Keep strip lights on, or switch them off?

Some people think that keeping strip lights on is cheaper and consumes less electricity than switching them on and off, because to restart these lights uses considerable electricity.

Restarting fluorescent tubes does require some energy, but only very little.

If you're going to be out of the room for more than a couple of minutes, switch them off.

- **Halogen bulbs** consume less electricity than conventional light bulbs, but they generally need to be used in larger numbers because each bulb only lights up a small area, so you may end up using more electricity.

- **Beware of 'uplighters'**: many consume a lot of electricity, using high-wattage bulbs of 300w or greater – that's the equivalent of over 30 low-energy light bulbs! Use energy-efficient spotlights instead.

- **Have candlelit suppers**.

LATER . . .

Energy-efficient light bulbs are cheap to run because they mainly make light rather than heat. 90% of the energy used by traditional bulbs is wasted in producing heat.

• **Buy and fit energy-efficient light bulbs** – they last about 12 times longer than ordinary bulbs and consume about 1/5 of the energy. They come in all shapes and sizes, including spotlights. Many energy companies and some councils are even giving them away.

If you do just one thing:
CHANGE TO ENERGY-EFFICIENT LIGHT BULBS

Cooking

COOKING

What has my cooking got to do with climate change?

- When you use gas or oil to cook with, carbon dioxide (CO_2) is produced; this is the main cause of climate change

- When you use electricity to cook with, the power station burned coal, gas or oil to produce that electricity – emitting CO_2 in the process

Less energy used for cooking = less CO_2

What can I do about it?

NOW...

Cookers are incredibly energy-hungry; an electric cooker with everything on uses about 11kWh (about £1.80) an hour.

- **Cut food into small pieces before cooking** – it will cook more quickly.

- **Select the correct saucepan size** for the heating element or gas flame.

- **Put a lid on top of the pan** when you can; your meal will cook much more quickly and you won't be wasting energy.

- **Turn down the heat** when a saucepan comes to the boil. You don't need as much heat to keep a pot boiling as you do to get it to the boil, and the contents will cook just as quickly.

- **Only use sufficient water to cover vegetables** when cooking them in saucepans.

- **Use a steamer for vegetables** – you can cook two or three vegetables on one element or gas ring.

- **Consider using a pressure cooker** for cooking some foods – it reduces cooking times dramatically.

- **Make one-pot meals** that only need one element or gas ring.

- **Use your oven efficiently** by filling up as much of the space as possible.

- **If you're cooking a meal in the oven**, don't be tempted to keep on opening the oven door to see how it's all going, as you lose a lot of heat doing this.

A fan-assisted electric oven warms up more quickly, distributes the heat more evenly, and uses about 20% less electricity than a conventional oven.

- **Cook two days' meals at once** in the oven and utilise the space. Reheating will use less energy than starting from scratch on day two.

- **Use the grill rather than the oven** when appropriate.

- **Food will cook more quickly on the top shelf** of a non-fan-assisted oven – it is much hotter than the bottom.

- **Use an electric kettle** to boil water for cooking.

- **Keep your kettle free of limescale** – it will be more efficient. Fill it with a mixture of 2/3 water and 1/3 vinegar and leave overnight. Rinse it out well, fill it with water, boil the water and throw it away.

- **Don't over-fill an electric kettle**: just put in the amount of water you want, but make sure you cover the element. You'll use less energy, it will cost less, and will come to the boil more quickly.

- **Make toast in a toaster** rather than under the grill if possible.

- **Plan ahead: get ready-made meals out of the freezer** early enough for them to defrost without using energy.

- **If you are in a hurry**, heat or defrost ready-made meals in a microwave rather than a conventional oven.

- **When cooking rice**, turn off the heat 5 minutes before the end of cooking time, keep the lid on and let it finish cooking in its own steam.

- **Compost all organic food waste** (see page 55).

LATER...

Electric kettles consume surprisingly large amounts of energy because they are used frequently, generally heat more water than is needed, and have to bring the water up to boiling point – an extremely energy-hungry process.

- **Get a 'slow cooker';** it's a really cheap way of cooking. The cooker gently simmers away all day, using little more power than a conventional light bulb

- **Electric kettles vary in the amount of electricity they consume;** when you need to replace yours, choose one with the minimum energy consumption

- **When replacing your electric oven,** consider a fan-assisted model – they are cheaper to run

- **Check out microwave ovens** – they consume about 80% less electricity than a conventional oven

If you do just one thing:
WHEN BOILING WATER IN A KETTLE, ONLY PUT IN AS MUCH WATER AS YOU NEED

KEEPING THINGS COOL

What have my fridge and freezer got to do with climate change?

- Electricity used for refrigeration and air conditioning units comes from power stations, most of which burn coal, gas or oil to produce it, emitting large quantities of CO_2 in the process.

Less electricity used for refrigeration = less CO_2

What can I do about it?

NOW ...

Fridges and freezers are never turned off – although they may not appear to use much energy, in an average home they are responsible for about 1/3 of the total electricity bill.

- **Wait until hot food has cooled down** before putting it into the fridge.
- **Don't keep the fridge door open** any longer than necessary.

- **Keep fridges and freezers well away from heat sources** such as cookers, dishwashers and washing machines.

- **If possible, site fridges and freezers out of direct sunlight**, as your appliance will use more energy trying to keep cool in the sun.

- **Try and keep your fridge and freezer full**; they will use less electricity.

- **Fill any empty spaces in your freezer** with scrunched-up paper or bubble wrap to stop warm air circulating when it is opened.

- **Defrost food** by putting it in the fridge the night before you want to use it. This will cool the fridge down and reduce its power consumption.

- **Keep the metal grids** (condenser coils) at the back of fridges and freezers **clean and dust-free**, and not jammed up against the wall; this allows the air to circulate more easily around them, and makes them more efficient.

- If you have a fitted kitchen with a built-in fridge or freezer, **make sure there is ample ventilation** to allow for air circulation around the condenser coils.

A chest freezer uses less electricity than a front-opening model because the cold air doesn't fall out every time the freezer is opened.

- **Defrost the fridge and freezer regularly**. If the ice inside gets more than 5mm thick, the appliances become inefficient.

- **Open the windows** instead of using an air-conditioning unit: air conditioning is extremely energy-hungry.

- **Draw your curtains or blinds in the heat of the day** to keep the sun out, to keep cool.

LATER . . .

- **Check the door seals on your fridge and freezer**: shut the door on a £5 note. If you can pull it out easily, or if your seals are damaged, they need replacing.

- **Consider buying an energy-efficient freezer** to replace an older appliance. You should recover the cost remarkably quickly.

- **If you are replacing your fridge**, remember that a new 'A++' energy-rated fridge consumes about 1/3 of the electricity of some of the older models.

- **Fit shutters or awnings on south-facing windows** to keep the sun out on very hot days.

If you do just one thing:
DON'T LEAVE THE FRIDGE DOOR OPEN LONGER THAN NECESSARY

WASHING DISHES

What has washing my dishes got to do with climate change?

- Energy used to run a dishwasher and heat its water comes from power stations which have burned coal, gas or oil to generate it, producing CO_2 in the process.

- Water companies also use energy to process and supply water to your home.

Less energy used for dishwashing = less CO_2

What can I do about it?

NOW...

If they are full and in economy mode, dishwashers can be more efficient than washing dishes by hand.

- **When washing dishes by hand**, fill a bowl with warm water and a little detergent, washing the 'cleaner' items first. Use cold water for rinsing. Don't wash up under a running tap.

- **If you use a dishwasher**, wait until it is full before using it. Don't be tempted by the 'half-load' facility, as it is nowhere near as energy-efficient.

- **Wash your pans up in the sink** – they take up a lot of room in the dishwasher.

- **Use the 'economy' or 'eco' programme** if your dishwasher has one; it will use less electricity and take less time.

- **Switch your dishwasher off completely when it has finished** – it is still consuming electricity on stand-by.

- If you **switch off the machine and open the door** when the dishwasher enters its **'drying phase'**, the dishes will dry naturally, **saving a considerable amount of energy.**

A water-efficient dishwasher will use as little as 15 litres per wash cycle, compared with some older models that use up to 50 litres.

LATER . . .

- When you buy a new appliance, get an 'AAA'-rated energy-efficient model; they cost less to run, save you money and contribute less to climate change.

If you do just one thing:
AVOID WASHING DISHES UNDER A RUNNING TAP

WASHING AND DRYING CLOTHES

What have washing and drying my clothes got to do with climate change?

- Electricity used for washing machines and tumble dryers comes from power stations which have burned coal, gas or oil to produce it, emitting CO_2 in the process.

- Water companies also use energy to process and supply water to your home.

Less clothes washing & tumble drying = less CO_2

What can I do about it?

NOW . . .

- **Consider washing some clothes less often** (e.g. jeans).

- **Hand-wash small items** of clothing in a bowl.

- **When washing clothes by hand**, there is no need to have the water hot. Most non-greasy dirt will wash out easily with cold water and detergent. Cold water is fine for rinsing your clothes afterwards.

- **Wait until you've got a full load** before using your washing machine – using the 'half load' programme does not save you half the energy, water or detergent.

Washing clothes at 60°C uses almost twice as much energy as a 40°C wash.

- **Use a lower temperature wash** for clothes which aren't very dirty: for most washes, 40°C is just as good as 60°C.

- **Use the economy programme** where possible.

- **If your machine has a cold wash option**, try using it for lightly soiled clothing. Most detergents work extremely well at low temperatures.

- **Connect both the hot and cold washing machine hoses** to your hot and cold water pipes, if you can. This will enable the machine to use readily available hot water, rather than having to heat cold water from scratch

- **Air-dry your clothes** on clothes racks or lines if possible – tumble dryers are very energy-hungry appliances.

- **If you have to use a tumble dryer**, then spin dry or wring the clothes before putting them in it. Clean out the 'fluff filter' every time you use the dryer: this improves the efficiency and your clothes will dry more quickly.

- **A water-efficient washing machine** will use as little as 45 litres per wash cycle, compared with some older models that use up to 100 litres.

- **Switch the tumble dryer off** when it has finished. It consumes almost 40% of the power whilst on stand-by!

LATER ...

- **If you live in a hard water area**, limescale on your washing machine element will reduce its efficiency. Every couple of months get rid of it by running the machine empty on a wash cycle using 200ml of white vinegar in the detergent tray. There are also de-scaling tablets available.

Energy-efficient washing machines use about 1/3 less electricity than older machines. The savings will more than cover the price of a new machine.

- **Get an 'AAA'-rated energy-efficient model** when you buy a new washing machine. They cost less to run, save you money and contribute less to climate change.

If you do just one thing:
USE A LOWER TEMPERATURE TO WASH YOUR CLOTHES

ELECTRICAL APPLIANCES AND ELECTRONIC GADGETS

What have my electrical appliances and electronic gadgets got to do with climate change?

- Electricity used to run electrical appliances and gadgets comes from power stations, which have burned coal, gas or oil to produce it, emitting CO_2 in the process

- Energy is used to make appliances and gadgets; the more we buy, the more energy is used to make our goods

Using appliances efficiently and switching them off after use = less CO_2

What can I do about it?

NOW ...

At any one time in most households, an average of 8 appliances are left on stand-by. In the average UK household, the TV is left on stand-by for more than 17 hours a day.

- **Turn off the chargers** for your mobile phone and laptop when not in use.

- **Turn off TVs, radios, stereos and computers** when not in use.

- **Set your computer to energy-saving mode** so that the screen is switched off if the computer has not been used for more than a few minutes.

- **Don't be fooled by screen-savers** – they use as much energy as the normal screen.

- **Set your computer to switch to 'stand-by' mode** when you aren't going to use it for a while. The power needed to restart is equivalent to the power used in only a few seconds of normal running time.

- **Turn your iron off** just before you finish ironing, and use the residual heat for the last few items of clothing.

A computer left on overnight uses 1 kWh of electricity; if 1,000 people turned off their computers overnight, they would save 180 tonnes of CO2 emissions every year.

- **Do a free energy check on your home** by visiting **www.energysavingtrust.org.uk**. You can reduce your energy consumption, knock hundreds of pounds off your energy bills, and cut down your CO2 emissions.

- **Use your electricity meter** to see for yourself which appliances use the most electricity: have a look at your meter whilst somebody else switches on kettles, toasters, tumble dryers, electric instant showers etc.

Most DVD players, video recorders and set-top boxes are never turned off. Even in stand-by mode some consume about 85% of the power that they use when working.

LATER . . .

- **Think about buying a small portable monitor** that shows you how much electricity you are using, how much it is costing, and the CO_2 you are adding to the atmosphere.

- **Buy a steam iron**: although they use slightly more electricity than dry irons, they are more efficient and take less time.

- **When replacing your computer**, compare overall energy use (both running and stand-by). Check that it has stand-by or power-down mode. Consider a laptop – they are more energy-efficient.

- Donate your old computer to a charity which renovates and recycles computers: see www.computer-aid.org.

If you do just one thing:
TURN OFF YOUR TV
WHEN NOT IN USE

RUBBISH

What's my rubbish got to do with climate change?

- Rubbish which is not recycled goes to landfill sites. Anything that decomposes in landfill sites will produce methane, a greenhouse gas which seeps into the atmosphere and is twenty one times more potent than CO_2.

- The more you buy, the more you throw away. The more new products you buy, the more CO_2 is created by the burning of coal, gas or oil to create energy for the manufacture of those goods.

- Transporting new goods around the world also produces CO_2.

Less rubbish = less greenhouse gases

What can I do about it?

- **Use your local recycling facility** to recycle anything not collected by your council: plastic, cans, glass, newspaper, wood, telephone directories, electronic goods, cardboard, batteries, electrical appliances and household goods can all be recycled.

- **Sell or donate things to a charity** rather than throwing them away.

> *Reduce: if you buy less, you will have less rubbish*
> *Reuse: if you reuse more, you will have less rubbish*
> *Recycle: if you recycle more, you will have less rubbish*

Batteries

- **Used batteries are hazardous waste** and must not go to landfill. Find out from your local council how to recycle or dispose of them. Use rechargeable ones where possible.

Cartons

- **If your council has a carton recycling facility**, use it!

Clothing

- **Don't be a slave to fashion** – the manufacture and transport of clothing causes CO_2 pollution.

- **Recycle through your local charity shops** or the textile bank at your recycling centre.

Computers

- **Rather than replacing your computer**, why not save money and upgrade it instead?

- **Give your old computer to a charity**. They will wipe the hard drive and donate it to developing countries

- **If you need to replace your computer**, look for the most energy-efficient model. Laptops are generally more energy-efficient.

Drinks cans

Making goods from recycled aluminium uses only 5% of the energy that is used in making new aluminium.

- **Recycling cans saves huge amounts of energy** – be sure to use your council's collection or local recycling facility.

Food

We throw away a third of all the food we buy in the UK.

- **Buy only what you need**.
- **Avoid 'By One Get One Free'** unless you can use or freeze the 'free' item.
- **Make a list and stick to it** – impulse-buying often leads to waste.

Every day 300,000 unopened meat-based, ready-made meals are thrown away in the UK.

- **Plan your shopping** so that you can use food before its 'sell by' and 'use by' dates, and find ways of using your leftover cooked food.

- **Pre-prepared meals are expensive**, and are the most frequently thrown away items.

Furniture

- **Unwanted furniture can be sold**, taken to charity shops or collected by your local furniture reuse network – see www.frn.org.uk.

Glass

- **Glass is a recycling success story**, which gets better and better. It is easy to recycle – either through your council collection or local bottle bank.

- **As well as being turned back into new bottles and jars**, glass can be recycled for many other uses, including fibreglass insulation materials and filtration material for water cleansing.

Ink cartridges

- **Consider using remanufactured cartridges**, or getting them refilled.

- **Don't send used cartridges to landfill** – recycle them through a charity using their Freepost envelopes.

There are over 30 million ink cartridges thrown away every year in the UK.

Mobile phones

- **When replacing an old mobile**, avoid sending it to landfill – recycle it. Many charities provide Freepost envelopes for this purpose.

- **If your mobile stops working, get it repaired.** There are many companies who will mend it at a very reasonable price.

In the UK, over 1,500 mobile phones are purchased every hour, and over 11 million are thrown away every year.

Nappies

- **'Disposable' nappies take hundreds of years to decompose in landfill sites.** Use reusable cloth nappies whenever possible, and pass them on for other babies to use when you have finished with them

8 million disposable nappies are thrown away every day in the UK.

Packaging

- **Where possible, avoid packaging** – particularly polystyrene, which almost always goes to landfill and is very difficult to recycle.

- **Try to recycle** any packaging you have.

- **Try to avoid pre-packaged food** – buy loose if possible.
- **Use your own shopping bags**.

Paper

- **Reuse and recycle paper**.
- **Use both sides**.
- **Make a pad from scrap paper**.
- **Reuse envelopes whenever possible** – many charities sell re-use labels.
- **Buy recycled paper goods wherever possible**, including recycled kitchen and loo rolls.
- **To reduce your junk mail**, register with the Mailing Preference Service – see **www.mpsonline.org.uk**.

Plastic

Almost 60% of all plastic waste is discarded packaging.

- **Waste plastic is a major problem** for the environment, with much of it ending up in landfill. It is derived from oil and CO_2 is emitted in the manufacturing process.
- **Refuse free plastic bags** – use your own cotton, hemp or jute bags instead.
- **Recycle through your council collection**, or at your local recycling centre.

- **Reuse plastic bags and recycle where possible** – many shops have a collection point.

Spectacles

- **You can donate your old specs** to an optician for reuse in the third world.

Start composting

Up to two-thirds of the average dustbin contents can be composted.

- **Making compost** lightens your dustbin and stops it smelling.

- **If you compost, less food is sent to landfill**, which in turn means that less noxious liquids (leachate) and less greenhouse gases – especially methane – are produced.

- **Home-made compost costs nothing** and is great for your garden. Used as mulch, it can reduce the amount of watering you need to do

- **Try a Bokashi system or a wormery** if you have no garden space:

  A Bokashi system uses bacteria that thrive without air to ferment the material. No unpleasant smells are produced, and it can be placed and used indoors

Wormeries – this system is great fun, but requires a little more effort. The worms within it need looking after, but it is most rewarding. The worms eat food waste, paper and cardboard, producing 'worm castes', a very valuable plant fertiliser. Once again, your local council might sell you one at a reduced price. There are many different types and sources

- **If you have some garden space**, you can use any of the following:

  Tumblers – available through some councils and large garden centres

  Green Johannas – the 'Rolls-Royce' of the plastic compost bin. The manufacturers claim you need no composting experience

  Digesters such as the 'Green Cone' dispose of kitchen waste, but do not produce compost.

If you do just one thing:
RECYCLE YOUR CANS

Travel

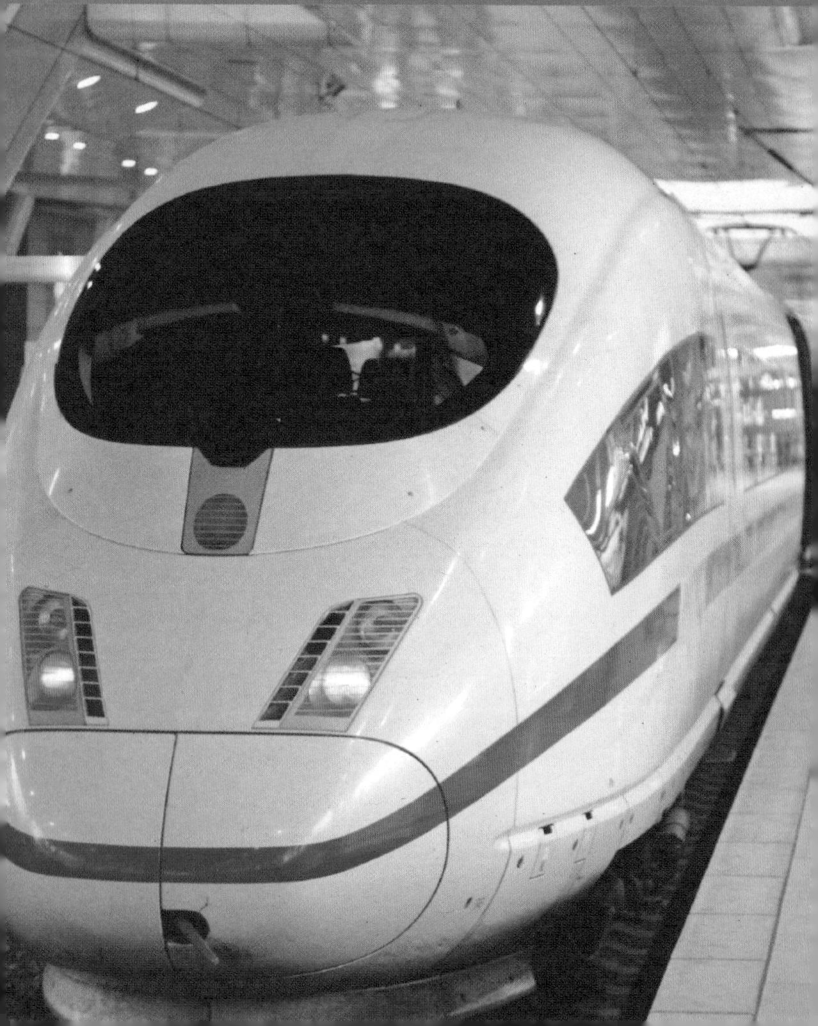

TRAVEL

What has my travel got to do with climate change?

- CO_2 is produced when petrol or diesel is used to power a car.

- Transport accounts for over 22% of CO_2 emissions, more than half of which comes from our cars.

- A journey by air creates about 10 times as much CO_2 as a similar journey by train.

Less driving and flying = less CO_2

What can I do about it?

NOW...

More than half of all car trips are under 3 miles, which would take about 10-15 minutes by bike.

- **Combine your activities** so that you reduce your car journeys.

- **Get out of your car** and on to a bus, train or bike.

- **Check out alternatives to your regular car journeys** – can you walk or go by bus?

- **Walk or cycle** part or all of the way when you can.

A fifth of all the cars on the road in the morning are taking children to school.

- **Get the children on bikes or walk with them to school** – avoid the school run.

- **Discover local cycle and walking routes**.

- **Share your car journey** with someone else.

- **Get together with other parents for the school run** – cut the number of cars at the school gate.

- **Avoid flying** – look for holiday destinations which you can reach by boat and train.

The effect of climate-changing exhaust gases from planes is around three times greater than emissions made at ground level.

- **Now we have a high-speed train link to Europe**, trains give a fast and environmentally-friendly way of travelling, are as quick as flying in many cases, and usually drop you in the middle of a city.

Your carbon footprint will be about ten times smaller if you travel by train rather than plane.

LATER . . .

- **Join a car club**.

- **Try to join a car pool or car share scheme** if you drive a journey regularly. See www.liftshare.org and www.carshare.com.

- **Arrange your work** to allow you to work from home occasionally if you can – even one day a week will dramatically reduce your journeys.

- **Start a car share** at work.

- **Plan your holidays without flying** – use www.seat61.com to plan your travel worldwide using trains and ships.

- **Buy the most fuel-efficient car** you can.

If you do just one thing:
REPLACE ONE CAR JOURNEY A WEEK WITH A GREENER WAY OF TRAVELLING

SHOPPING

What has my shopping got to do with climate change?

- Everything you buy has an effect on your carbon footprint – the amount of CO_2 your lifestyle generates.

- Your choice of household appliances also affects your carbon footprint; some are more energy-efficient than others, both in their manufacture and their use.

- The kind of food and clothing you buy makes a difference. Artificial fertilisers and pesticides, used to grow most food and cotton, are derived from oil, and their manufacture is energy-intensive and emits CO_2.

- When you buy anything made of timber from non-sustainable forests there is an additional impact on your carbon footprint. Trees are the 'lungs' of our world – they transform CO_2 into oxygen, thereby reducing the amount of CO_2 in the atmosphere.

- The number of miles your goods have travelled to get from their source to your home makes a difference. The greater the distance, the greater the CO_2 emitted, especially if they have been transported by air

- Shopping trips by car add CO_2 to the atmosphere

Buying locally produced products = less CO_2

What can I do about it?

NOW . . .

- **Buy locally grown food, in season**, from your local food shops.

   Almost 2/3 of the apples sold in supermarkets are air-freighted from abroad.

- **Reduce your food miles** – avoid food which has travelled a long way to reach you.

- **Buy organic if possible**: organic food and clothing will have been grown without the use of artificial fertilizers and pesticides.

- **Buy furniture made from natural timber** that has come from a sustainable source. Look out for FSC (Forest Stewardship Council) or PEFC (Programme for the Endorsement of Forest Certification) symbols.

- **Buy the most energy-efficient household appliances**.

- **Shop online** and get your goods delivered.

- **Plan your shopping** so that you do as much in one trip as possible.

- **Use a bike or the bus** for your shopping trips where possible.

- **Share a car** – shop with a friend.

- **Buy second-hand** if you can.

- **Buy goods that will last**.

- **Buy less!**

LATER . . .

- **Start a local food co-operative** – reduce your shopping trips.

- **Grow your own fruit and vegetables** in window boxes, tubs or your back garden – zero food miles!

- **Try to get an allotment** if you want to grow more.

If you do just one thing:
BUY LOCAL

Water

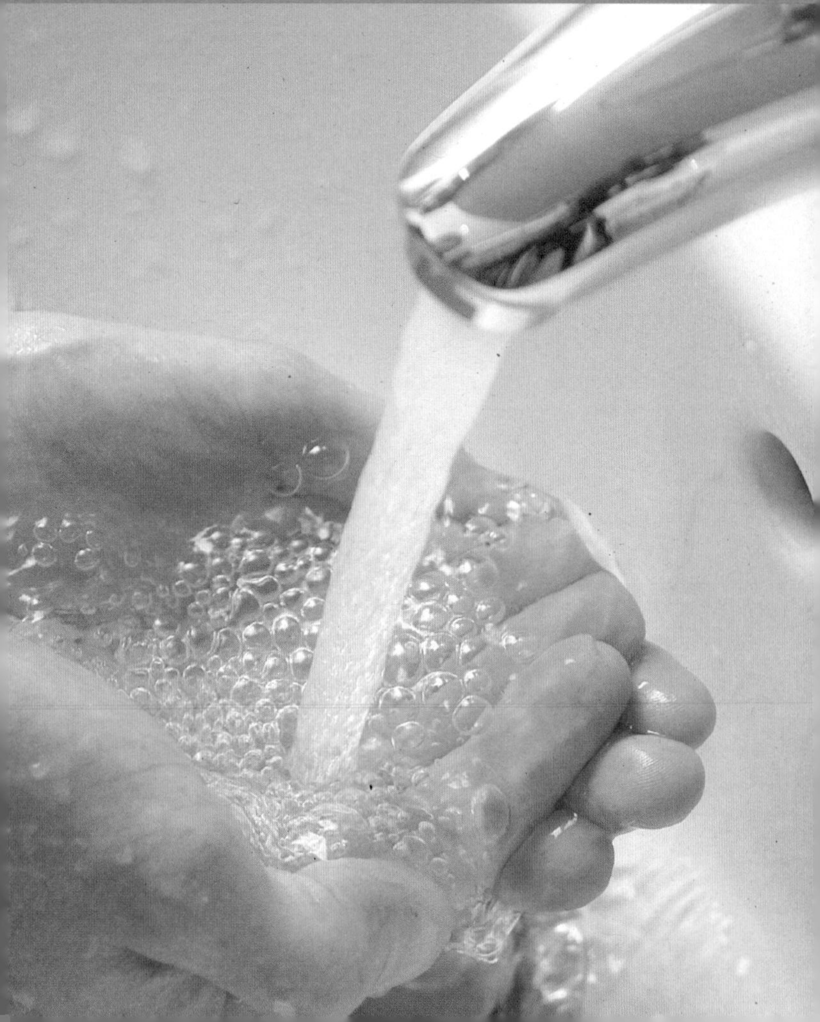

WATER

What's my water got to do with climate change?

- Collecting, treating and pumping water for use in your home uses energy.

- That energy has been produced in a power station which burned coal, gas or oil to produce it, emitting CO_2 in the process.

- Our wetlands are drying out releasing CO_2 which has been locked away for thousands of years.

Less water used = less CO_2

How much water do you use?

Bath	80 litres
5 minute shower (not power shower)	35 litres
5 minute power shower	90 litres
Brushing teeth with tap running	6 litres/min
Brushing teeth with tap off	1 litre
One toilet flush	9 litres
Other water use (drinking, cooking etc.)	25 litres
Washing machine	60 litres
Dishwasher	40 litres
Washing car with bucket	10 litres
Hosepipe/sprinkler	540 litres/hour

What can I do about it?

NOW...

We use 70% more water today than we did 40 years ago.

- **Work out how much water you use**. Can you reduce that amount and save money at the same time?

- **Never leave a tap running**.

- **Don't keep the tap running** whilst cleaning your teeth; use a mug of water – a running tap can use as much as 10 litres of water in the time it takes to clean your teeth.

- **Have a shower instead of a bath**. But if you use a power shower, beware: they can use as much water as a bath if you shower for more than five minutes.

- **Fix any leaky taps**.

One dripping tap can waste at least 5,500 litres of water a year.

- **Avoid using sprinklers and garden hoses**, and use a watering can as much as possible – a garden hose or sprinkler can use almost as much water in an hour as an average family of four uses in one day.

- **Collect the water from your roof** in a water butt or two.

- **Use a bowl to wash vegetables** or to wash and rinse plates.

- **Use the left-over water** to water your garden or house plants, providing it is not too soapy.

Overall, only about 3% of the water entering the average home is actually used as 'drinking' water.

- **Store drinking water in a jug in the fridge**, rather than waiting for the tap to run cold.

- **Bottled water has to be packaged** and travels many miles. Try chilling tap water in the fridge and see if you can taste the difference!

About 95% of the water that gets delivered to our houses goes down the drain.

- **Only use a dishwasher or washing machine** if you have a full load. If you just have a few things to wash, use a bowl.

- **Wash your car at home** with a sponge and bucket, rather than at a car wash.

LATER ...

- *Get a dual-flush loo* which enables you to choose a short flush most of the time, using a large flush only when necessary. Many people in the world exist on 10 litres of water day or less – we can use almost that amount in one flush of the toilet!

- **If you have an old toilet**, you can reduce the amount of water it uses by fitting a free water-saving 'HIPPO', 'Save-a-flush' or 'Hog Bag' in your cistern. Contact your water company to get one free: see
www.hippo-the-watersaver.co.uk
www.save-a-flush.co.uk.

Over a quarter of all the clean, drinkable water you use in your home is used to flush the toilets.

- **If you replace a loo**, choose a slimline model, rather than a full size toilet; they use a lot less water per flush.

- **Put a gutter and water butt** on your greenhouse or garden shed.

- **Fit a flow regulator** to your shower.

- **Fit water-saving taps**.

- **Use your 'grey water'** (waste water from baths, sinks, etc): attach a hosepipe to your washing machine outlet pipe and collect the used water when the machine is discharging. If your bath is one or more floors above the garden, collect your used bath water as well – siphon it into a water butt for use on your flowers. 'Grey water' can be used to water your garden flowers, but not vegetables as it can contain faecal coliforms, which might cause illness if ingested.

- **Insulate all outside taps and pipes** to prevent the water freezing inside them when it is cold, causing burst or leaking pipes..

- **Have a water meter installed** – you will certainly use less water, and installation is free.

- **Install a rainwater harvesting system** – see www.rainwaterharvesting.co.uk.

If you do just one thing:
TURN OFF THE TAP

Gardening

GARDENING

What has my gardening got to do with climate change?

- Using artificial fertilisers and pesticide in your garden increases the amount of CO_2 in the atmosphere. Fertilisers and pesticides are derived from oil, and their manufacture is very energy-intensive.

- Water companies use energy to extract, treat and pump water to your home. The less water you use, the less energy is used, and therefore less greenhouse gases are produced.

- Watering your garden using mains water adds to your carbon footprint.

- Both petrol-driven and electrical garden implements add CO_2 to the atmosphere, either directly (if petrol driven) or indirectly via the power station.

More water butts = less CO_2

What can I do about it?

NOW...

- **Go organic** – feed your soil with natural fertilisers, e.g. horse manure or compost.

- **Feed your plants with natural feed**, e.g. seaweed extract.

- **Use natural pest control**: for example, spray a mixture made with water and eco-friendly washing-up liquid on aphids.

- **Use a watering can** rather than a sprinkler or hose – you will use less water.

The average roof collects about 85,000 litres of rain a year! This could fill 450 water butts with free water.

- **Collect the rainwater from your roof** in a water butt (or two).

- **Retain moisture in your soil by mulching** round the base of plants. You can make a mulch using organic materials such as manure, hay or straw, a thin layer of grass cuttings, or locally produced bark or wood chippings.

Water is in greatest demand in the heat of summer, when over 70% of the water supply can be being used for watering gardens.

- **Plant close together** to conserve water in the soil.

- **Choose drought-resistant plants**, flowers and shrubs that positively enjoy dry, hot conditions, such as evening primrose, buddleia, rockrose, thyme and lavender.

- **Keep your gutters clear of leaves**.

- **Make compost** (see pages 55-56). Instead of throwing away all your garden waste, vegetable peelings, paper and cardboard, compost them. You can use the compost to form a layer of mulch on top of the soil, which will keep it cool and help reduce moisture loss. Making compost helps to lock carbon up in your soil, which means less CO_2 emissions, and compost in soil acts like a sponge, holding onto water and nutrients and reducing the need to water and fertilise.

- **Leave the lawn longer** – save on water and leave your mower in the shed!

- **Don't water the lawn** – it will recover when it rains again.

A garden hose or sprinkler can use almost as much water in an hour as an average family of four uses in one day.

LATER . . .

- **Install water butts** to collect the rainwater from your roof.

- **Check out a push mower** – new models are lightweight and easy to use.

- **Consider using 'grey water'** – waste water from baths, the kitchen sink etc, to water the flowers in your garden, but avoid grey water that has a lot of strong detergents in it, as this might damage your plants.

- **Grow food instead of grass**.

- **Plant vegetables** amongst your flowers.

- **Plant a tree**.

- **Vegetables such as sweetcorn, broad beans and French beans** will survive with less watering, although their yields will be smaller.

- **Root crops** such as beetroot, turnips and carrots, together with asparagus, are the most drought-resistant, but root crops will become hard and woody if they get too dry.

- **Crops with plenty of leaves,** such as lettuce, peas, runner beans, tomatoes, potatoes, salad onions, cauliflower and broccoli, require the most water.

- **Marrows, courgettes and cucumbers** need regular watering once their fruit begins to swell.

- **Don't water your plants little and often,** as this encourages shallow rooting. Do it occasionally but thoroughly, which will make them more resistant to drought.

- **Direct the water to the base of the plants** and give their roots a good soak. A couple of times a week should be sufficient even when the weather is hot.

If you do just one thing:
COLLECT WATER FROM YOUR ROOF IN A WATER BUTT

Renewable energy and your home

RENEWABLE ENERGY

- Renewable energy is energy produced by a source that continually renews itself. Well-known sources are the sun, moving water, wind and plant materials. This energy can be used for space heating and hot water heating, and to produce electricity for your home.

- By using renewable energy instead of conventional energy sources, you can reduce the amount of CO_2 your household produces. This will reduce your contribution to climate change and save you a considerable amount of money once installed, as most of these energy sources will provide endless free energy, and reduce the impact on your household of gas and electricity price rises.

- Providing you have already taken some basic steps to reduce your energy consumption, there will probably be grants available to help you pay for the purchase and installation of a renewable energy system. These grants can be quite substantial.

When considering the purchase and installation of a renewable energy system, you need to consider:

- **The suitability of your home** Do you have a south-facing roof or wall? Is your house exposed to the wind?

- **Payback** (the amount of time it takes for the renewable energy system to pay for itself). This varies considerably according to which system you install.

- **Initial cost** Some systems are dramatically cheaper than others to buy and install.

Solar power

- **Energy from the sun** can be used both to provide domestic hot water and to produce electricity for your home. Different technologies are used for each.

To produce domestic hot water

- **Solar heating panels** use the sun's energy to heat domestic hot water. This energy typically reduces your water heating bill by 65%–75%.

- **Solar heating systems** work in conjunction with your conventional domestic hot water system.

- **Most south-facing roofs, walls or gardens** are suitable for the installation of solar heating panels.

To produce electricity

- **Photovoltaic (PV) cells** convert sunlight to electricity. This electricity is fed into the mains grid, thereby reducing your electricity bill. The PV cells can be put on a south-facing roof or wall, provided that they are strong enough to support the additional weight and are not shaded by trees or other buildings.

Small-scale wind turbines

To produce electricity

- **Wind turbines** convert the energy of moving wind into electricity. For many houses in the UK, a new kind of micro-turbine that attaches to your chimney or roof is the most convenient and practical.

- **The electricity produced** by micro wind turbines is fed back into the mains electricity grid, thereby reducing your electricity bill. Your house needs in an exposed position to make this system suitable for you.

Biomass (biofuels)

To heat your house and hot water

- **Biomass or biofuels** are materials such as wood or straw which grow quickly and can be burned to release heat for space heating and domestic hot water. Biomass is different from all the other renewable energy sources because the fuel generally has to be purchased.

Biomass is a renewable energy source because:

- **The materials are quick to grow**, absorbing CO_2 in the process.

- **The CO_2 released** when it is burned **balances the CO_2** which was absorbed during the growth of the material, effectively making the process carbon-neutral.

- **Wood (in the form of logs or pellets)** is the most commonly used biofuel. It should be burned in an efficient, controllable manner, either in stand-alone stoves or in boilers.

Ground source heat pumps

To heat your house and hot water

- **Heat pumps take heat from several metres under the ground** (which remains at about $12°C$ all year round) and use it to heat your house – just like a refrigerator in reverse.

- **They can also be used to warm water** before it enters your domestic hot water heater, thereby saving on energy used. If you want to install a heat pump, you will need sufficient space outside to dig either a trench or a borehole.

- **Heat pumps very efficient**, although they are run by electricity: for every unit of electricity used to run the heat pump, about four units of heat energy are created.

Small-scale hydro power

To produce electricity

- **If you have a fast-moving stream or river** running near your house, it might be possible to generate electricity from the moving water. Though not the simplest of renewable energy systems to install, hydro schemes have the capacity to generate substantial amounts of electricity, which can then be sold to your electricity company.

- **The cost of hydro power schemes** varies hugely according to the size of the project, but they can sometimes offer high returns. The potential source of power will need to be assessed before any other steps are taken.

- **Consider forming a community hydro project**, if you think your local river has the potential to generate electricity. There are people operating successful schemes who are willing to provide advice.

Energy Labels

All new household appliances must display an energy label. Use these to help you choose the more energy-efficient models and save you money.

All products are rated from 'A' to 'G' (with 'A' being the most efficient). Some appliances now offer even higher efficiency ratings, such as 'A+' and 'A++'.

Refrigerators, freezers and fridge-freezer combinations

Look for 'A+' or 'A++' energy labels; the better the energy rating, the less it will cost to run. 'A++' fridges and freezers use one third less electricity than an 'A'-rated model.

Washing machines

These have three ratings given: for Energy Efficiency, Washing Performance and Spin Drying Performance. Purchase 'AAA'-rated machines if possible. A few manufacturers now have an 'A+' rating for their energy efficiency – look out for these.

Dishwashers

These appliances also have three ratings: for Energy Efficiency, Washing Performance and Drying Performance. Purchase 'AAA'-rated machines if possible.

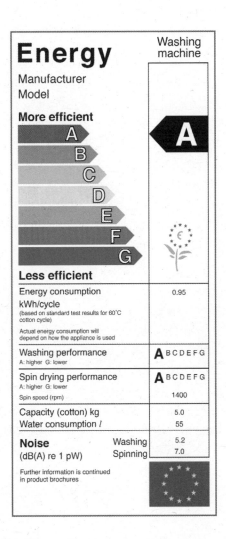

Resources

RESOURCES

WEBSITES

Carshare

A directory of UK car-sharing sites, enabling both drivers and passengers to find travel companions and share travel costs.
www.carshare.com

Community Composting Network (CCN)

Assists communities with their composting projects – from small groups of allotment holders to council kerbside collections.
☎ 0114 2580 483
www.communitycompost.org

Community Recycling Network (CRN)

Helps you to find your nearest community waste recyclers, and to get advice on running a community waste project.
☎ 0117 942 0142
www.crn.org.uk

Computer Aid international

Donate your unwanted computers to Computer Aid, who will refurbish them and send them to third world countries for reuse.
www.computer-aid.org
☎ 020 7281 0091

DirectGov

The website of the UK government. Use it to find the contact details of your local authority. Contact them to see if what grants or special offers are available.
www.direct.gov.uk

Energy Efficiency Advice Centre

For informative, independent advice on the energy and water efficiency of washing and dishwasher machines.
☎ 0845 727 7200
www.energysavingtrust.org.uk

Energy Future

A website that aims to clear away confusion and dispel the myths and misconceptions about topics such as climate change and DIY energy – and more.
www.energyfuture.org.uk

The Energy Saving Trust (EST)

Provides independent advice and information about energy efficiency, insulation and renewable energy options, and the availability of grants.
www.energysavingtrust.org.uk

Furniture Re-use Network (FRN)

The national co-ordinating body for 400 furniture and appliance re-use and recycling organisations in the UK, which collect a wide range of household items to pass on to people in need.
www.frn.org.uk

The Forest Stewardship Council (FSC)

Promotes responsible management of the world's forests and gives accreditation to products manufactured from virgin materials sourced from well managed forests.
www.fsc-uk.org

Green Electricity Marketplace

Information on electricity companies offering green electricity tariffs in your area, with the facility to switch online for some tariffs.
www.greenelectricity.org

Liftshare

Enables both drivers and passengers to find travel companions and share travel costs.
www.liftshare.org

The Mailing Preference Service

Enables individuals and organisations to reduce junk mail.
www.mpsonline.org.uk

The National Energy Foundation

An independent educational charity working for a more efficient, innovative and safe use of energy, and to increase the public awareness of energy in all its aspects. Currently it is working in the areas of renewable energy and energy efficiency.
☎ 01908 665555
www.nef.org.uk

Programme for Endorsement of Forestry Certification schemes (PEFC)

A global umbrella organisation for schemes that certify timber and other tree products.
www.pefc.org

Recycle More

Helps you to find your nearest recycling point, and provides resources and advice on recycling.
☎ 020 7321 3500
www.recycle-more.co.uk

The Recycling Helpline

☎ 0800 435576
This number will put you through to your local council's helpline. The Recycle Now campaign is an independent, government-funded organisation which provides advice on recycling.
www.recyclenow.com

Seat Sixty-One

Enables you to plan your worldwide travel using trains and ships instead of flying.
www.seat61.com

Vehicle Certification Agency (VCA)

Helps anyone buying a new car to choose a model which has the least impact on the environment, and provides information on new car fuel consumption and exhaust emissions.
www.vcacarfueldata.org.uk

WasteOnline

Provides information on sustainability, resource use and waste issues.
www.wasteonline.org.uk

Women's Environmental Network (WEN)

A campaign group informing both women and men on environmental issues.
☎ 020 7481 9004
www.wen.org.uk

Waste and Resources Action Programme (WRAP)

Good site for advice on home composting, food waste and recycling.
☎ 01295 819614
www.wrap.org.uk

Other Green Books Guides:

Water: use less – save more
by Jon Clift and Amanda Cuthbert
100 water-saving tips for the home, in full colour.
£4.95 paperback

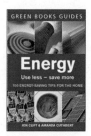

Energy: use less – save more
by Jon Clift and Amanda Cuthbert
100 energy-saving tips for the home, in full colour.
£4.95 paperback

Reduce, Reuse, Recycle: an easy household guide
by Nicky Scott
An easy-to-use A–Z household guide to recycling.
£4.95 paperback

Other Green Books Guides:

Composting: an easy household guide
by Nicky Scott
Tells you everything you need to know for
successful home composting.
£4.95 paperback

Cutting Your Car Use
by Anna Semlyen
Tackle car dependency and change your
travel habits.
£4.95 paperback

Cycling to Work: a beginner's guide
by Rory McMullan
Gives support and encouragement to get
to work by bike.
£4.95 paperback

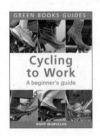

Other Green Books Guides:

Greening Your Office: From cupboard to corporation, an A–Z guide
by Jon Clift and Amanda Cuthbert
Packed with ideas for making your office eco-friendly.
£4.95 paperback

Green Up! An A–Z of environmentally friendly home improvements
by Will Anderson
A compact, clear and straightforward reference guide to greening your house.
£7.95

Ecology Begins at Home
by Archie Duncanson
Offers inspiring and environmentally friendly options that don't necessarily require major changes to your lifestyle.
£4.95

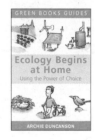

Other Green Books Guides:

Eat Well, Waste Less: An A–Z guide to using up leftovers
by Bish Muir
Shows you how to plan your shopping, reduce waste, and use up your leftover food to make delicious meals, save money and reduce your carbon footprint.
£4.95

Also available from Green Books:

Diary of an Eco-Builder
by Will Anderson
An inspirational account of the challenges of building your own eco-house.
£10.95

**Organic Gardening:
The Natural No-Dig Way**
by Charles Dowding
Discover the true potential of your garden with this back-to-basics approach to successful gardening.
£10.95